50 Gourmet Grilling Recipes for Summer

By: Kelly Johnson

Table of Contents

- Grilled Lemon-Herb Chicken Skewers
- Spicy Grilled Shrimp Tacos with Avocado Salsa
- Honey-Balsamic Glazed Salmon
- Grilled Vegetable Platter with Chimichurri Sauce
- Stuffed Portobello Mushrooms with Goat Cheese
- Herbed Lamb Chops with Garlic and Rosemary
- Grilled Peach Salad with Burrata
- Korean BBQ Beef Short Ribs
- Charred Corn on the Cob with Parmesan and Lime
- Grilled Eggplant and Zucchini Stack with Feta
- Cedar Plank Salmon with Dill and Lemon
- Buffalo Cauliflower Steaks with Blue Cheese Dressing
- Moroccan-Spiced Grilled Chicken Thighs
- Cilantro-Lime Grilled Pork Chops
- Grilled Asparagus with Balsamic Glaze
- Pineapple Teriyaki Chicken Burgers
- Grilled Lamb Kofta with Tzatziki Sauce
- Mediterranean Grilled Shrimp and Quinoa Salad
- Chipotle BBQ Grilled Meatballs
- Grilled Caprese Salad with Balsamic Reduction
- Smoky BBQ Brisket Sandwiches
- Stuffed Bell Peppers with Quinoa and Black Beans
- Grilled Lobster Tail with Garlic Butter
- Tequila Lime Grilled Shrimp Skewers
- Cilantro Pesto Grilled Chicken Breast
- Saffron-Grilled Scallops with Citrus Salsa
- Garlic and Herb Grilled Artichokes
- Spiced Grilled Tofu with Peanut Sauce
- Smoky Grilled Watermelon Salad
- Grilled Thai Pork Satay with Peanut Sauce

- Charred Brussels Sprouts with Bacon
- Sundried Tomato and Basil Grilled Chicken
- Grilled Sausages with Sauerkraut and Mustard
- Raspberry-Balsamic Glazed Grilled Duck Breast
- Grilled Romaine Salad with Caesar Dressing
- Herb-Crusted Grilled Flank Steak
- Grilled Veggie Flatbread with Hummus
- Orange-Honey Grilled Carrots
- Grilled Fajitas with Marinated Steak and Peppers
- Ginger-Lime Grilled Shrimp with Avocado
- Moroccan Grilled Vegetable Skewers
- Stuffed Grilled Avocados with Tuna Salad
- Lemon-Thyme Grilled Chicken with Pesto
- Grilled Garlic Shrimp with Linguine
- Smoked Paprika Grilled Cornish Hen
- Pork Tenderloin with Maple-Mustard Glaze
- Grilled Pizza with Fresh Basil and Mozzarella
- Barbecue Grilled Eggplant with Tahini Sauce
- Grilled Tuna Steaks with Soy Ginger Marinade
- Blackened Grilled Catfish with Remoulade Sauce

Grilled Lemon-Herb Chicken Skewers

Ingredients:

- 1 lb chicken breast, cubed
- 2 tablespoons olive oil
- Juice of 1 lemon
- 2 teaspoons dried oregano
- 2 cloves garlic, minced
- Salt and pepper to taste
- Skewers (soaked in water if wooden)

Instructions:

1. In a bowl, mix olive oil, lemon juice, oregano, garlic, salt, and pepper.
2. Add chicken cubes to the marinade and let sit for at least 30 minutes.
3. Preheat the grill to medium-high heat.
4. Thread the marinated chicken onto skewers.
5. Grill for 10-12 minutes, turning occasionally, until cooked through.

Spicy Grilled Shrimp Tacos with Avocado Salsa

Ingredients:

- 1 lb shrimp, peeled and deveined
- 2 tablespoons olive oil
- 1 tablespoon chili powder
- 1 teaspoon cumin
- Salt to taste
- 8 small corn tortillas
- 1 avocado, diced
- 1/2 cup diced tomatoes
- 1/4 cup red onion, diced
- Juice of 1 lime

Instructions:

1. In a bowl, toss shrimp with olive oil, chili powder, cumin, and salt.
2. Preheat the grill to medium-high heat.
3. Grill shrimp for 2-3 minutes on each side until pink and cooked through.
4. In a separate bowl, mix avocado, tomatoes, onion, lime juice, and salt to make salsa.
5. Serve grilled shrimp in corn tortillas topped with avocado salsa.

Honey-Balsamic Glazed Salmon

Ingredients:

- 4 salmon fillets
- 1/4 cup balsamic vinegar
- 2 tablespoons honey
- 1 tablespoon olive oil
- Salt and pepper to taste

Instructions:

1. In a small saucepan, combine balsamic vinegar and honey. Cook over medium heat until thickened (about 5 minutes).
2. Preheat the grill to medium-high heat.
3. Brush salmon fillets with olive oil and season with salt and pepper.
4. Grill salmon for 4-5 minutes per side, brushing with the balsamic glaze during the last few minutes of cooking.

Grilled Vegetable Platter with Chimichurri Sauce

Ingredients:

- 1 zucchini, sliced
- 1 bell pepper, sliced
- 1 eggplant, sliced
- 1 cup cherry tomatoes
- 2 tablespoons olive oil
- Salt and pepper to taste
- Chimichurri sauce (store-bought or homemade)

Instructions:

1. Preheat the grill to medium-high heat.
2. Toss vegetables with olive oil, salt, and pepper.
3. Grill vegetables for 5-7 minutes, turning occasionally until tender and charred.
4. Serve grilled vegetables drizzled with chimichurri sauce.

Stuffed Portobello Mushrooms with Goat Cheese

Ingredients:

- 4 large portobello mushrooms
- 4 oz goat cheese, softened
- 1/4 cup breadcrumbs
- 2 cloves garlic, minced
- 2 tablespoons olive oil
- Fresh herbs (thyme or parsley), chopped

Instructions:

1. Preheat the grill to medium heat.
2. In a bowl, mix goat cheese, breadcrumbs, garlic, herbs, salt, and pepper.
3. Brush mushroom caps with olive oil and fill each with the cheese mixture.
4. Grill mushrooms for 5-7 minutes, until cheese is melted and mushrooms are tender.

Herbed Lamb Chops with Garlic and Rosemary

Ingredients:

- 8 lamb chops
- 2 tablespoons olive oil
- 2 cloves garlic, minced
- 2 teaspoons fresh rosemary, chopped
- Salt and pepper to taste

Instructions:

1. In a bowl, mix olive oil, garlic, rosemary, salt, and pepper.
2. Coat lamb chops with the herb mixture and let marinate for at least 30 minutes.
3. Preheat the grill to medium-high heat.
4. Grill lamb chops for 4-5 minutes per side for medium-rare doneness.

Grilled Peach Salad with Burrata

Ingredients:

- 2 ripe peaches, halved and pitted
- 1 tablespoon olive oil
- 4 cups mixed greens
- 8 oz burrata cheese
- 1/4 cup balsamic glaze
- Salt and pepper to taste

Instructions:

1. Preheat the grill to medium-high heat.
2. Brush peach halves with olive oil and grill for 3-4 minutes until grill marks appear.
3. In a bowl, combine mixed greens, grilled peaches, and burrata cheese.
4. Drizzle with balsamic glaze and season with salt and pepper before serving.

Enjoy these delicious grilled recipes!

Korean BBQ Beef Short Ribs

Ingredients:

- 2 lbs beef short ribs
- 1/2 cup soy sauce
- 1/4 cup brown sugar
- 1/4 cup rice vinegar
- 1 tablespoon sesame oil
- 4 cloves garlic, minced
- 1 inch ginger, grated
- 2 green onions, chopped

Instructions:

1. In a bowl, mix soy sauce, brown sugar, rice vinegar, sesame oil, garlic, ginger, and green onions.
2. Marinate beef short ribs in the mixture for at least 4 hours, preferably overnight.
3. Preheat the grill to medium-high heat.
4. Grill the marinated short ribs for 5-7 minutes per side until cooked to desired doneness.

Charred Corn on the Cob with Parmesan and Lime

Ingredients:

- 4 ears of corn, husked
- 2 tablespoons olive oil
- 1/2 cup grated Parmesan cheese
- Juice of 1 lime
- Salt and pepper to taste

Instructions:

1. Preheat the grill to medium-high heat.
2. Brush corn with olive oil and season with salt and pepper.
3. Grill corn for 10-15 minutes, turning occasionally until charred.
4. Remove from grill and brush with lime juice, then sprinkle with Parmesan cheese.

Grilled Eggplant and Zucchini Stack with Feta

Ingredients:

- 1 eggplant, sliced
- 2 zucchini, sliced
- 1/4 cup olive oil
- Salt and pepper to taste
- 1 cup crumbled feta cheese
- Fresh basil for garnish

Instructions:

1. Preheat the grill to medium heat.
2. Brush eggplant and zucchini slices with olive oil and season with salt and pepper.
3. Grill vegetables for 4-5 minutes per side until tender and charred.
4. Stack grilled vegetables, sprinkle with feta cheese, and garnish with fresh basil.

Cedar Plank Salmon with Dill and Lemon

Ingredients:

- 1 lb salmon fillet
- 1 cedar plank (soaked in water for at least 1 hour)
- Juice of 1 lemon
- 2 tablespoons olive oil
- 2 tablespoons fresh dill, chopped
- Salt and pepper to taste

Instructions:

1. Preheat the grill to medium heat.
2. Place soaked cedar plank on the grill and heat for 5 minutes until it starts to smoke.
3. Rub salmon with olive oil, lemon juice, dill, salt, and pepper.
4. Place salmon on the cedar plank and grill for 12-15 minutes until cooked through.

Buffalo Cauliflower Steaks with Blue Cheese Dressing

Ingredients:

- 1 large cauliflower, sliced into thick steaks
- 1/4 cup olive oil
- 1/2 cup buffalo sauce
- Salt and pepper to taste
- Blue cheese dressing for serving

Instructions:

1. Preheat the grill to medium heat.
2. Brush cauliflower steaks with olive oil and season with salt and pepper.
3. Grill cauliflower for 5-7 minutes per side until tender and charred.
4. Brush with buffalo sauce and grill for an additional 1-2 minutes.
5. Serve with blue cheese dressing.

Moroccan-Spiced Grilled Chicken Thighs

Ingredients:

- 4 chicken thighs, boneless and skinless
- 2 tablespoons olive oil
- 1 tablespoon Moroccan spice blend (cumin, coriander, paprika, cinnamon)
- Salt and pepper to taste
- Fresh cilantro for garnish

Instructions:

1. In a bowl, mix olive oil, Moroccan spice blend, salt, and pepper.
2. Coat chicken thighs in the mixture and marinate for at least 30 minutes.
3. Preheat the grill to medium-high heat.
4. Grill chicken thighs for 6-7 minutes per side until cooked through.
5. Garnish with fresh cilantro before serving.

Cilantro-Lime Grilled Pork Chops

Ingredients:

- 4 pork chops
- 1/4 cup olive oil
- Juice of 2 limes
- 1/4 cup chopped cilantro
- 2 cloves garlic, minced
- Salt and pepper to taste

Instructions:

1. In a bowl, whisk together olive oil, lime juice, cilantro, garlic, salt, and pepper.
2. Marinate pork chops in the mixture for at least 30 minutes.
3. Preheat the grill to medium-high heat.
4. Grill pork chops for 5-6 minutes per side until cooked through.

Enjoy these delicious grilled recipes!

Grilled Asparagus with Balsamic Glaze

Ingredients:

- 1 lb asparagus, trimmed
- 2 tablespoons olive oil
- Salt and pepper to taste
- 1/4 cup balsamic glaze

Instructions:

1. Preheat the grill to medium-high heat.
2. Toss asparagus with olive oil, salt, and pepper.
3. Grill asparagus for 5-7 minutes until tender and slightly charred.
4. Drizzle with balsamic glaze before serving.

Pineapple Teriyaki Chicken Burgers

Ingredients:

- 1 lb ground chicken
- 1/4 cup teriyaki sauce
- 1/2 cup crushed pineapple, drained
- 1/4 cup breadcrumbs
- Salt and pepper to taste
- Pineapple slices for grilling

Instructions:

1. In a bowl, mix ground chicken, teriyaki sauce, crushed pineapple, breadcrumbs, salt, and pepper.
2. Form mixture into patties.
3. Preheat the grill to medium heat and grill patties for 6-7 minutes per side.
4. Grill pineapple slices for 2-3 minutes per side until caramelized.
5. Serve burgers with grilled pineapple on buns.

Grilled Lamb Kofta with Tzatziki Sauce

Ingredients:

- 1 lb ground lamb
- 2 cloves garlic, minced
- 1 tablespoon ground cumin
- 1 tablespoon ground coriander
- 1 teaspoon cinnamon
- Salt and pepper to taste
- 1/2 cup Greek yogurt
- 1/2 cucumber, grated
- 1 tablespoon lemon juice

Instructions:

1. In a bowl, combine ground lamb, garlic, cumin, coriander, cinnamon, salt, and pepper.
2. Form into kebabs and skewer.
3. Preheat the grill to medium-high heat and grill kofta for 5-7 minutes per side.
4. For tzatziki, mix yogurt, grated cucumber, and lemon juice in a bowl.
5. Serve kofta with tzatziki sauce.

Mediterranean Grilled Shrimp and Quinoa Salad

Ingredients:

- 1 lb shrimp, peeled and deveined
- 1/4 cup olive oil
- 2 tablespoons lemon juice
- 1 teaspoon oregano
- Salt and pepper to taste
- 1 cup cooked quinoa
- 1 cup cherry tomatoes, halved
- 1/2 cucumber, diced
- 1/4 cup feta cheese, crumbled

Instructions:

1. In a bowl, mix shrimp, olive oil, lemon juice, oregano, salt, and pepper.
2. Preheat the grill to medium-high heat and grill shrimp for 2-3 minutes per side until pink and cooked.
3. In a serving bowl, combine quinoa, cherry tomatoes, cucumber, and feta cheese.
4. Top with grilled shrimp before serving.

Chipotle BBQ Grilled Meatballs

Ingredients:

- 1 lb ground beef or turkey
- 1/2 cup breadcrumbs
- 1/4 cup chopped cilantro
- 1 tablespoon chipotle sauce
- 1 egg
- Salt and pepper to taste
- BBQ sauce for brushing

Instructions:

1. In a bowl, mix ground meat, breadcrumbs, cilantro, chipotle sauce, egg, salt, and pepper.
2. Form into meatballs.
3. Preheat the grill to medium heat and grill meatballs for 8-10 minutes, turning occasionally and brushing with BBQ sauce.

Grilled Caprese Salad with Balsamic Reduction

Ingredients:

- 2 large tomatoes, sliced
- 8 oz fresh mozzarella, sliced
- Fresh basil leaves
- 1/4 cup balsamic reduction
- Olive oil, for drizzling

Instructions:

1. Preheat the grill to medium heat.
2. Grill tomato and mozzarella slices for 1-2 minutes per side until slightly charred.
3. On a platter, layer grilled tomatoes and mozzarella, and add fresh basil.
4. Drizzle with balsamic reduction and olive oil before serving.

Smoky BBQ Brisket Sandwiches

Ingredients:

- 2 lbs brisket
- 1/4 cup smoked paprika
- 1 tablespoon garlic powder
- Salt and pepper to taste
- BBQ sauce for serving
- Buns for serving

Instructions:

1. Rub brisket with smoked paprika, garlic powder, salt, and pepper.
2. Preheat the grill to medium heat and grill brisket for 4-5 hours, turning occasionally until tender.
3. Slice brisket and serve on buns with BBQ sauce.

Enjoy these flavorful grilled recipes!

Stuffed Bell Peppers with Quinoa and Black Beans

Ingredients:

- 4 bell peppers, halved and seeds removed
- 1 cup cooked quinoa
- 1 can (15 oz) black beans, rinsed and drained
- 1 cup corn (fresh or frozen)
- 1 teaspoon cumin
- 1 teaspoon chili powder
- Salt and pepper to taste
- 1 cup shredded cheese (optional)

Instructions:

1. Preheat the oven to 375°F (190°C).
2. In a bowl, mix cooked quinoa, black beans, corn, cumin, chili powder, salt, and pepper.
3. Stuff the bell pepper halves with the quinoa mixture and place them in a baking dish.
4. If using, sprinkle cheese on top.
5. Bake for 25-30 minutes until the peppers are tender.

Grilled Lobster Tail with Garlic Butter

Ingredients:

- 2 lobster tails
- 4 tablespoons unsalted butter, melted
- 2 cloves garlic, minced
- Juice of 1 lemon
- Salt and pepper to taste

Instructions:

1. Preheat the grill to medium-high heat.
2. Cut the lobster tails in half lengthwise and remove the meat slightly from the shell.
3. In a bowl, mix melted butter, garlic, lemon juice, salt, and pepper.
4. Brush the lobster meat with the garlic butter mixture.
5. Grill the lobster tails for 5-7 minutes, basting with more butter, until cooked through.

Tequila Lime Grilled Shrimp Skewers

Ingredients:

- 1 lb shrimp, peeled and deveined
- 1/4 cup tequila
- Juice of 2 limes
- 2 tablespoons olive oil
- 2 cloves garlic, minced
- Salt and pepper to taste

Instructions:

1. In a bowl, combine tequila, lime juice, olive oil, garlic, salt, and pepper.
2. Add shrimp to the marinade and let sit for 30 minutes.
3. Preheat the grill to medium-high heat and thread shrimp onto skewers.
4. Grill shrimp for 2-3 minutes per side until pink and cooked.

Cilantro Pesto Grilled Chicken Breast

Ingredients:

- 4 boneless, skinless chicken breasts
- 1 cup fresh cilantro
- 1/4 cup olive oil
- 1/4 cup nuts (pine nuts or walnuts)
- 2 cloves garlic
- Salt and pepper to taste

Instructions:

1. In a food processor, blend cilantro, olive oil, nuts, garlic, salt, and pepper until smooth.
2. Marinate chicken breasts in cilantro pesto for at least 30 minutes.
3. Preheat the grill to medium-high heat and grill chicken for 6-7 minutes per side until cooked through.

Saffron-Grilled Scallops with Citrus Salsa

Ingredients:

- 1 lb scallops
- 1/4 teaspoon saffron threads
- 2 tablespoons olive oil
- Salt and pepper to taste
- 1 orange, diced
- 1 grapefruit, diced
- 1 tablespoon chopped fresh mint

Instructions:

1. Preheat the grill to medium-high heat.
2. Soak saffron in 1 tablespoon of warm water for 5 minutes.
3. In a bowl, mix scallops with saffron water, olive oil, salt, and pepper.
4. Grill scallops for 2-3 minutes per side until opaque.
5. Serve with a salsa made of diced orange, grapefruit, and mint.

Garlic and Herb Grilled Artichokes

Ingredients:

- 4 artichokes, halved and trimmed
- 1/4 cup olive oil
- 2 cloves garlic, minced
- 1 tablespoon fresh lemon juice
- Salt and pepper to taste

Instructions:

1. Preheat the grill to medium heat.
2. Steam artichokes for 20-25 minutes until tender.
3. In a bowl, mix olive oil, garlic, lemon juice, salt, and pepper.
4. Brush the mixture onto the artichokes and grill for 5-7 minutes until charred.

Spiced Grilled Tofu with Peanut Sauce

Ingredients:

- 14 oz firm tofu, drained and pressed
- 2 tablespoons soy sauce
- 1 tablespoon sesame oil
- 1 tablespoon chili paste
- 1/2 cup peanut butter
- 1/4 cup coconut milk
- 1 tablespoon lime juice

Instructions:

1. Slice tofu into 1-inch thick slabs.
2. Marinate tofu in soy sauce, sesame oil, and chili paste for at least 30 minutes.
3. Preheat the grill to medium heat and grill tofu for 4-5 minutes per side until grill marks appear.
4. In a bowl, mix peanut butter, coconut milk, and lime juice for the sauce.
5. Serve grilled tofu with peanut sauce drizzled on top.

Enjoy these delicious stuffed and grilled recipes!

Smoky Grilled Watermelon Salad

Ingredients:

- 4 cups watermelon, cut into wedges
- 2 tablespoons olive oil
- 1 teaspoon smoked paprika
- Salt and pepper to taste
- 1 cup feta cheese, crumbled
- Fresh mint leaves for garnish

Instructions:

1. Preheat the grill to medium-high heat.
2. In a bowl, toss watermelon wedges with olive oil, smoked paprika, salt, and pepper.
3. Grill watermelon for 2-3 minutes on each side until charred.
4. Remove from the grill, let cool slightly, then top with feta cheese and mint leaves.

Grilled Thai Pork Satay with Peanut Sauce

Ingredients:

- 1 lb pork tenderloin, sliced into thin strips
- 2 tablespoons soy sauce
- 1 tablespoon brown sugar
- 1 tablespoon curry powder
- 1/2 cup coconut milk
- 1/2 cup peanut butter
- 1 tablespoon lime juice

Instructions:

1. In a bowl, mix soy sauce, brown sugar, curry powder, and coconut milk to create a marinade.
2. Add pork strips to the marinade and let sit for at least 30 minutes.
3. Preheat the grill to medium heat and thread pork onto skewers.
4. Grill for 3-4 minutes per side until cooked through.
5. In another bowl, mix peanut butter and lime juice for the sauce. Serve grilled pork with peanut sauce.

Charred Brussels Sprouts with Bacon

Ingredients:

- 1 lb Brussels sprouts, halved
- 4 slices bacon, chopped
- 2 tablespoons olive oil
- Salt and pepper to taste

Instructions:

1. Preheat the grill to medium-high heat.
2. In a bowl, toss Brussels sprouts with bacon, olive oil, salt, and pepper.
3. Place Brussels sprouts in a grill basket and grill for 10-12 minutes, tossing occasionally until charred and crispy.

Sundried Tomato and Basil Grilled Chicken

Ingredients:

- 4 boneless, skinless chicken breasts
- 1/2 cup sundried tomatoes, chopped
- 1/4 cup fresh basil, chopped
- 1/4 cup olive oil
- Salt and pepper to taste

Instructions:

1. In a bowl, mix sundried tomatoes, basil, olive oil, salt, and pepper.
2. Marinate chicken breasts in the mixture for at least 30 minutes.
3. Preheat the grill to medium-high heat and grill chicken for 6-7 minutes per side until cooked through.

Grilled Sausages with Sauerkraut and Mustard

Ingredients:

- 4 sausages (your choice)
- 2 cups sauerkraut, drained
- Mustard for serving

Instructions:

1. Preheat the grill to medium heat.
2. Grill sausages for 5-7 minutes, turning occasionally until browned and cooked through.
3. Serve sausages topped with sauerkraut and a side of mustard.

Raspberry-Balsamic Glazed Grilled Duck Breast

Ingredients:

- 2 duck breasts
- 1/2 cup raspberries
- 1/4 cup balsamic vinegar
- 2 tablespoons honey
- Salt and pepper to taste

Instructions:

1. Preheat the grill to medium-high heat.
2. In a saucepan, combine raspberries, balsamic vinegar, honey, salt, and pepper. Simmer until reduced.
3. Score the skin of the duck breasts and season with salt and pepper.
4. Grill duck breasts, skin side down, for 6-8 minutes until crispy. Flip and grill for another 4-5 minutes until cooked to your liking.
5. Drizzle raspberry-balsamic glaze over grilled duck before serving.

Grilled Romaine Salad with Caesar Dressing

Ingredients:

- 2 heads romaine lettuce, halved
- 2 tablespoons olive oil
- Salt and pepper to taste
- 1/2 cup Caesar dressing
- Croutons and Parmesan cheese for serving

Instructions:

1. Preheat the grill to medium-high heat.
2. Brush cut sides of romaine lettuce with olive oil and season with salt and pepper.
3. Grill lettuce for 2-3 minutes until charred.
4. Drizzle with Caesar dressing and top with croutons and Parmesan cheese before serving.

Enjoy these flavorful grilled recipes!

Herb-Crusted Grilled Flank Steak

Ingredients:

- 1 lb flank steak
- 2 tablespoons olive oil
- 2 tablespoons fresh rosemary, chopped
- 2 tablespoons fresh thyme, chopped
- 2 cloves garlic, minced
- Salt and pepper to taste

Instructions:

1. Preheat the grill to high heat.
2. In a bowl, mix olive oil, rosemary, thyme, garlic, salt, and pepper.
3. Rub the herb mixture all over the flank steak and let it marinate for at least 30 minutes.
4. Grill steak for about 4-5 minutes on each side for medium-rare, or until desired doneness.
5. Let rest for a few minutes before slicing against the grain.

Grilled Veggie Flatbread with Hummus

Ingredients:

- 4 pieces flatbread
- 1 zucchini, sliced
- 1 bell pepper, sliced
- 1 red onion, sliced
- Olive oil for drizzling
- 1 cup hummus
- Fresh parsley for garnish

Instructions:

1. Preheat the grill to medium heat.
2. Toss vegetables with olive oil, salt, and pepper.
3. Grill vegetables for about 5-7 minutes until tender and charred.
4. Spread hummus over flatbread and top with grilled vegetables.
5. Garnish with fresh parsley before serving.

Orange-Honey Grilled Carrots

Ingredients:

- 1 lb carrots, peeled and halved lengthwise
- 2 tablespoons honey
- Juice of 1 orange
- Salt and pepper to taste

Instructions:

1. Preheat the grill to medium heat.
2. In a bowl, mix honey, orange juice, salt, and pepper.
3. Toss carrots in the mixture and let marinate for 10-15 minutes.
4. Grill carrots for about 10-15 minutes, turning occasionally, until tender and caramelized.

Grilled Fajitas with Marinated Steak and Peppers

Ingredients:

- 1 lb flank steak
- 2 bell peppers, sliced
- 1 onion, sliced
- 1/4 cup olive oil
- Juice of 2 limes
- 1 tablespoon chili powder
- 1 teaspoon cumin
- Salt and pepper to taste

Instructions:

1. In a bowl, mix olive oil, lime juice, chili powder, cumin, salt, and pepper.
2. Marinate the flank steak in the mixture for at least 1 hour.
3. Preheat the grill to high heat and grill steak for about 5 minutes per side for medium-rare.
4. Grill bell peppers and onions until tender.
5. Slice steak and serve with grilled vegetables in tortillas.

Ginger-Lime Grilled Shrimp with Avocado

Ingredients:

- 1 lb shrimp, peeled and deveined
- 2 tablespoons olive oil
- Juice of 2 limes
- 2 tablespoons fresh ginger, grated
- Salt and pepper to taste
- 2 avocados, halved

Instructions:

1. In a bowl, mix olive oil, lime juice, ginger, salt, and pepper.
2. Add shrimp and marinate for 20-30 minutes.
3. Preheat the grill to medium-high heat and grill shrimp for 2-3 minutes on each side until pink and opaque.
4. Serve shrimp on top of halved avocados.

Moroccan Grilled Vegetable Skewers

Ingredients:

- 1 zucchini, cubed
- 1 bell pepper, cubed
- 1 red onion, cubed
- 1 cup cherry tomatoes
- 2 tablespoons olive oil
- 1 tablespoon Moroccan spice blend

Instructions:

1. Preheat the grill to medium heat.
2. In a bowl, toss vegetables with olive oil, Moroccan spice blend, salt, and pepper.
3. Thread vegetables onto skewers.
4. Grill for about 10-12 minutes, turning occasionally, until charred and tender.

Stuffed Grilled Avocados with Tuna Salad

Ingredients:

- 2 avocados, halved and pitted
- 1 can tuna, drained
- 1/4 cup mayonnaise
- 1 tablespoon Dijon mustard
- Salt and pepper to taste
- Juice of 1 lime

Instructions:

1. Preheat the grill to medium heat.
2. In a bowl, mix tuna, mayonnaise, mustard, lime juice, salt, and pepper.
3. Grill avocado halves, cut side down, for 3-4 minutes until slightly charred.
4. Fill grilled avocado halves with tuna salad and serve.

Enjoy these delicious grilled recipes!

Lemon-Thyme Grilled Chicken with Pesto

Ingredients:

- 4 chicken breasts
- 2 tablespoons olive oil
- Juice of 1 lemon
- 2 teaspoons fresh thyme, chopped
- Salt and pepper to taste
- 1/2 cup pesto for serving

Instructions:

1. In a bowl, mix olive oil, lemon juice, thyme, salt, and pepper.
2. Marinate chicken breasts in the mixture for at least 30 minutes.
3. Preheat the grill to medium-high heat and grill chicken for about 6-7 minutes on each side until cooked through.
4. Serve with pesto drizzled on top.

Grilled Garlic Shrimp with Linguine

Ingredients:

- 1 lb shrimp, peeled and deveined
- 4 cloves garlic, minced
- 1/4 cup olive oil
- Juice of 1 lemon
- 8 oz linguine, cooked
- Fresh parsley for garnish

Instructions:

1. In a bowl, mix shrimp, garlic, olive oil, lemon juice, salt, and pepper.
2. Preheat the grill to medium heat and grill shrimp for 2-3 minutes on each side until pink.
3. Toss cooked linguine with grilled shrimp and garnish with fresh parsley before serving.

Smoked Paprika Grilled Cornish Hen

Ingredients:

- 2 Cornish hens
- 2 tablespoons olive oil
- 1 tablespoon smoked paprika
- 1 teaspoon garlic powder
- Salt and pepper to taste

Instructions:

1. Preheat the grill to medium heat.
2. In a bowl, mix olive oil, smoked paprika, garlic powder, salt, and pepper.
3. Rub the mixture over the hens and let marinate for 30 minutes.
4. Grill hens for about 30-35 minutes, turning occasionally, until cooked through.

Pork Tenderloin with Maple-Mustard Glaze

Ingredients:

- 1 lb pork tenderloin
- 1/4 cup maple syrup
- 2 tablespoons Dijon mustard
- Salt and pepper to taste

Instructions:

1. Preheat the grill to medium-high heat.
2. In a bowl, mix maple syrup, Dijon mustard, salt, and pepper.
3. Brush the mixture over the pork tenderloin.
4. Grill for about 20-25 minutes, turning occasionally, until the internal temperature reaches 145°F.

Grilled Pizza with Fresh Basil and Mozzarella

Ingredients:

- 1 pizza dough
- 1 cup marinara sauce
- 8 oz fresh mozzarella, sliced
- Fresh basil leaves
- Olive oil for drizzling

Instructions:

1. Preheat the grill to medium heat.
2. Roll out the pizza dough and grill one side until slightly charred.
3. Flip the dough, spread marinara sauce, and top with mozzarella.
4. Grill until the cheese is melted and bubbly, about 5-7 minutes.
5. Top with fresh basil and drizzle with olive oil before serving.

Barbecue Grilled Eggplant with Tahini Sauce

Ingredients:

- 2 eggplants, sliced
- Olive oil for brushing
- Salt and pepper to taste
- 1/2 cup tahini sauce for drizzling

Instructions:

1. Preheat the grill to medium heat.
2. Brush eggplant slices with olive oil and season with salt and pepper.
3. Grill eggplant for about 5-6 minutes on each side until tender and charred.
4. Drizzle with tahini sauce before serving.

Grilled Tuna Steaks with Soy Ginger Marinade

Ingredients:

- 2 tuna steaks
- 1/4 cup soy sauce
- 1 tablespoon ginger, grated
- 1 tablespoon olive oil
- Salt and pepper to taste

Instructions:

1. In a bowl, mix soy sauce, ginger, olive oil, salt, and pepper.
2. Marinate tuna steaks in the mixture for 20-30 minutes.
3. Preheat the grill to high heat and grill tuna steaks for about 2-3 minutes on each side for medium-rare.

Blackened Grilled Catfish with Remoulade Sauce

Ingredients:

- 4 catfish fillets
- 2 tablespoons blackening seasoning
- Olive oil for brushing
- 1/2 cup remoulade sauce for serving

Instructions:

1. Preheat the grill to high heat.
2. Brush catfish fillets with olive oil and coat with blackening seasoning.
3. Grill catfish for about 4-5 minutes on each side until cooked through.
4. Serve with remoulade sauce on the side.

Enjoy these flavorful grilled recipes!